ECCE HOMO

GEORGE GROSZ

ECCE HOMO

JACK BRUSSEL NEW YORK 1965

MANUFACTURED IN THE UNITED STATES OF AMERICA
Printed on Curtis Rag Paper. Type set by Polyglot Press. Watercolor
Reproduction by Rose Color Labs., Inc. Drawings and Text Printed by
Mahoney and Roese, Inc. Bound by H. Wolff Book Manufacturing Co.

ECCE HOMO

Issued in Three States Limited to One Thousand Copies
The Sixteen Watercolors and Eighty-Four Drawings
The Sixteen Watercolors in a Portfolio with the Introduction
The Eighty-Four Drawings with the Introduction

EIGHTY-FOUR DRAWINGS

SIXTEEN WATERCOLORS

INTRODUCTION
BY LEE REVENS

By an irony that has not passed unnoticed, the immensity of the second World War has never managed to dispossess the 1914-1918 smaller-scale devastation from its logically nullified title, "The Great War." This instance of vocabulary lag in popular usage is actually a folk-wise testimonial to a profound truth: The Great War was a catastrophic warning that placid, smug, self-esteeming Western society had to detach itself from its illusions, and face up to the contemptuous reality—it had not advanced all that much beyond its caveman ancestry.

That we did not take that prodigiously over-loud signal seriously, but played Lord of the Flies children games at the peace conference and thereafter, inevitably led to Fascism, Hitler, the second World War, and the Cold War that, if we are lucky, will go on forever.

But some sleepers who were wakened in 1914 did not return to bed, did not pull the covers up over their heads. Instead, these few, eyes once opened, toured the streets and institutions, and reported, as sharply as graphics and words permit, the realities behind the comforting illusions, the skeletons behind the pebbled-glass doors, the truth behind the trivializing facades.

George Grosz is perhaps pre-eminent among this handful of wakened prophets who became wakers. And this portfolio from his most passionate years, mercilessly communicating his perceptions and insights, from 1918 to 1922, must be ranked with the biblical, alas futile, voices of Jeremiah, Isaiah and John, forewarning, goading, exposing—and failing to make a difference in the outcome.

Let it not become a question of art criticism—tracing influences, from Zille, to Masereel, or parallelisms with Otto Dix and Klee, or noting successors, and derivatives like Gluyas Williams, Herb Block, and Mauldin. Here, the essence is the timeless appropriateness, the annihilating accuracy, the devastating judiciousness of George Grosz in graphic commentary on a sector of Twentieth Century society that twice contrived to destroy millions of human beings, irrevocably distort and wreck the lives of hundreds of millions more,—and incalculably set back the course of human progress that was winding slowly upward from the tribal values of brutally primitive, selfish goals, in a long, infinitesimally slow advance towards rational, humane and dignified living for all mankind.

A worker with words, not knowing that George Grosz had written a magnificently articulate autobiography, ("A Little Yes and a Big No") would acknowledge him a master of language, based on the brief captions that, so inspired in their appropriateness, add new precision and proliferating implications to the naked power of the drawings. The nearly irresistible temptation to spell out their meanings in multiplying examples and analogies, is a prime measure of the psychological and sociological commentary Grosz has densely packed into each petrification of a moment in our history. Consider the hopelessness of adequately demarking the range of commentaries, if given the archeologist assignment of reconstructing the era from just this collection (a temptingly plausible tour de force). Just note, for example, that the Wagnerian knight is bare-assed, in the apt evocation of the two-year old who mindlessly resumes his game for the few moments his mother is getting a clean diaper to replace the soiled one she has just removed (60). Or contemplate the glory-conscious pride of the smug types at their outing on their national holiday (43). Or what does the psychiatrist do with "Trio" (74); the sociologist with "Cross-Section" (49) and "Suburb" (73); the economist with "Closing Time" (45)?

In leafing through—in coming to rapt stop on any page—remember that all this was before Hitler had raised the Nazis to one seat in the

Reichstag; before Coolidge had succeeded Harding; before radio had entered the home; or solo flights bridged the Atlantic. Grosz, without blinders, tried to tell us what we were—and lived to be exiled from his native land when the evils he had exposed in the egg became the cocks of the barnyard.

Have people changed? Has society moved onward to humane, co-operative, rational solutions of universal problems? We have the Salk vaccine—and the tactical atomic warhead. We have the 35 hour week (being reduced to 30, 25 and even 20 hours by automation already in pilot plant use)—and we see the German rocket scientist arming Nasser; De Gaulle rejecting European unity; and China pledging to hand out atom bombs to nations who fought with bows and spears within this century.

George Grosz (and the Great War) were detonating alarms. But perhaps mankind is meant to sleep through, covers over the head, to its thermonuclear extinction. This re-issue of his master-work, validated by the bitter mockeries of forty years, might just possibly strike a nerve, here and there. It might just possibly add a recruit to the tiny ranks of those that believe it better to see clearly and take lucid steps no matter how painful than to postulate (simultaneously) the wild contradictions that our fellow men are advanced humanists, and that the ratio of over-kill is our only safeguard.

One very minor comment on a personal relation to Grosz and this volume. As an adolescent, encountering some of these drawings in various art and sociological works (that reproduced them singly to point a moral or trace a trend) I was inescapably taken by the profound dimension added by the simple notion of making street garments transparent. The concept of stripping the veil and revealing actuality is, of course, obviously a part of it. But at that age, I faintly recognized something that perhaps retains validity. Grosz confronts us with the fact that our minds are compartmentalized. All of us know the creature that lives within our clothes—yet all of us accept our fellow mortals as if they were born clothed, and might be other creatures than us. The incessant *demonstration that we are all naked creatures, only incidently wearing garments, effectively brings home the heart truth: deal with others as with ourselves; accept the fact of mankind's limited, mortal, earthy, material existence. Be not at all deceived into translating the use of clothing to the possession of a high level of ethic, or a guarantee of civilized behavior. Be, at all times, as real in your thinking about your fellow man, his capacities and his limitations, as you are of your own. Project his humanness, when you deal with him, but remember to project as firmly his frailties. This is not cynicism, but rationalness. Start with what you know he is, metaphorically and actually underneath, and there is at least the hope that you will talk sense to each other, manage honestly, understand humanly, and cope realistically.*

This, to challenge his sardonic despair, is perhaps, the hopeful message we can find in Grosz—over-riding, underlying, and animating the brilliant (and once again) accurate portraits he paints of us. This he superbly epitomizes in the heretical title that mocks the connotations of two thousand years of theology, that laughs down the evolutionist's optimism, and confounds the humanist's ethical piety. Look here, not elsewhere, to—BEHOLD MAN!

September 1965   LEE REVENS

ECCE HOMO

2

3

6

II

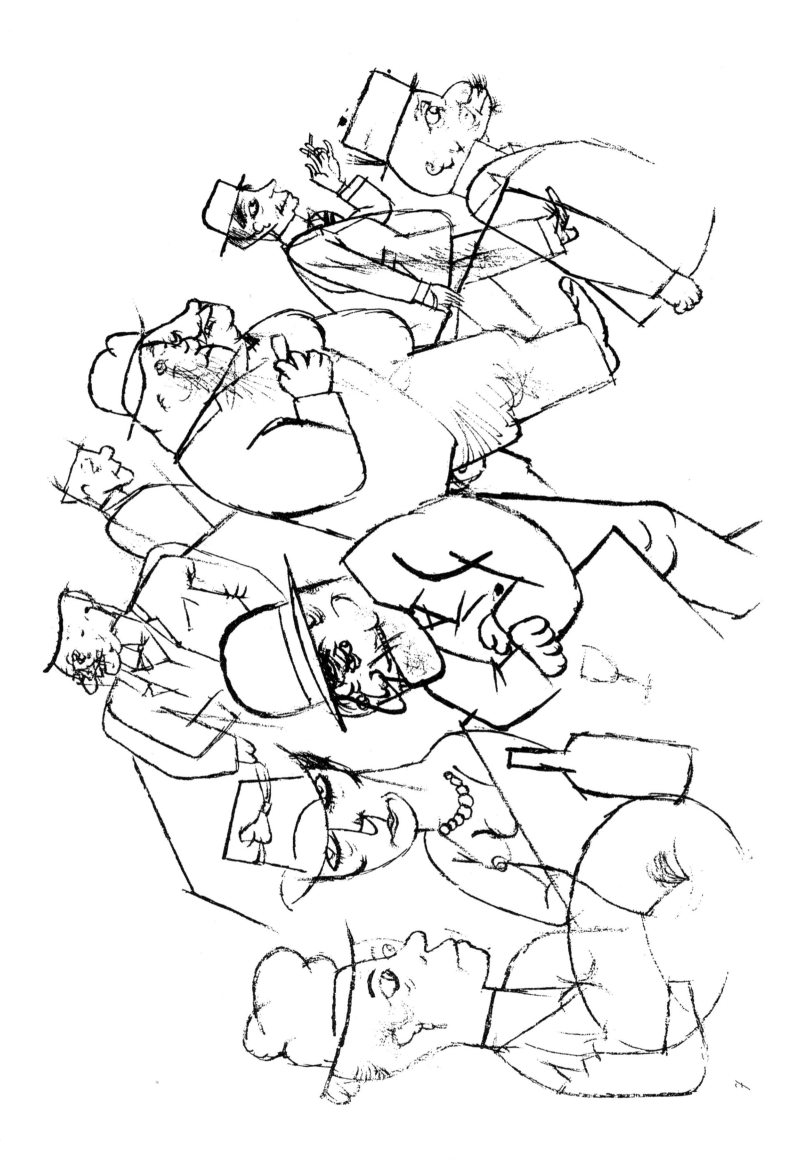

9

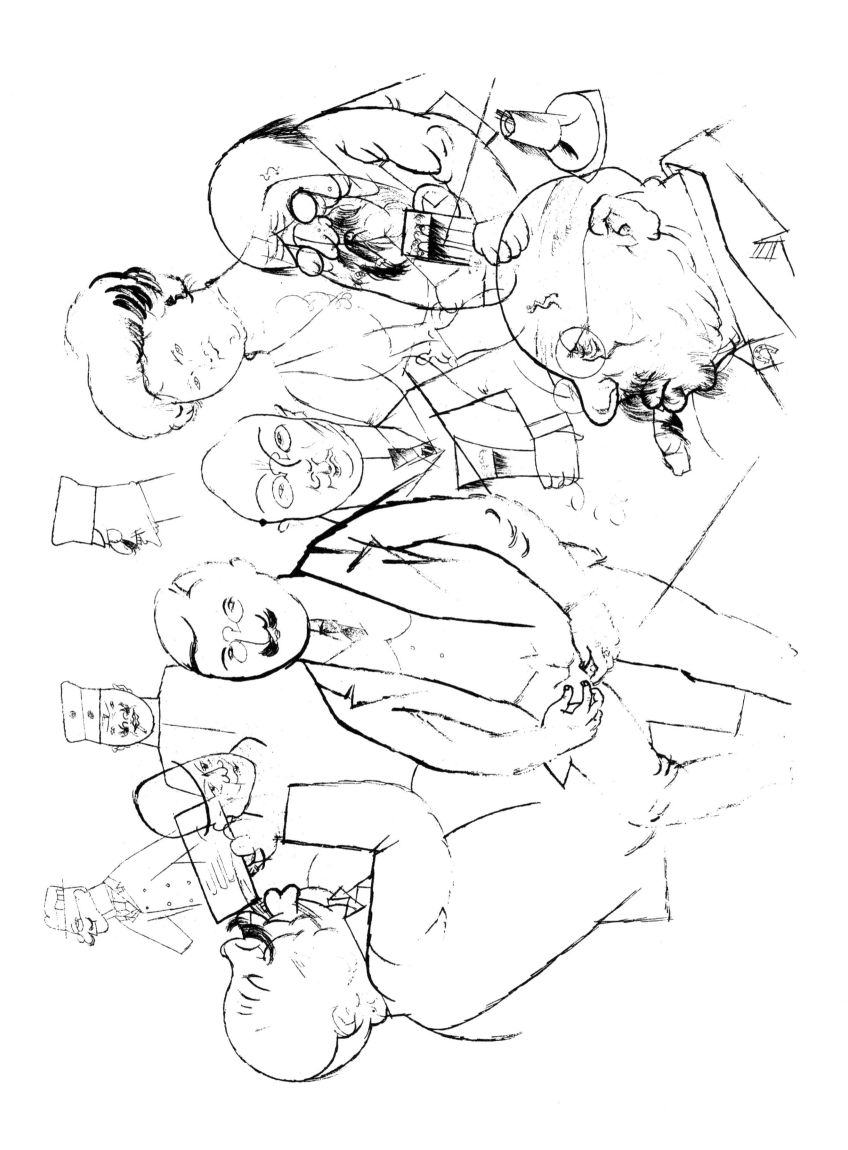

III

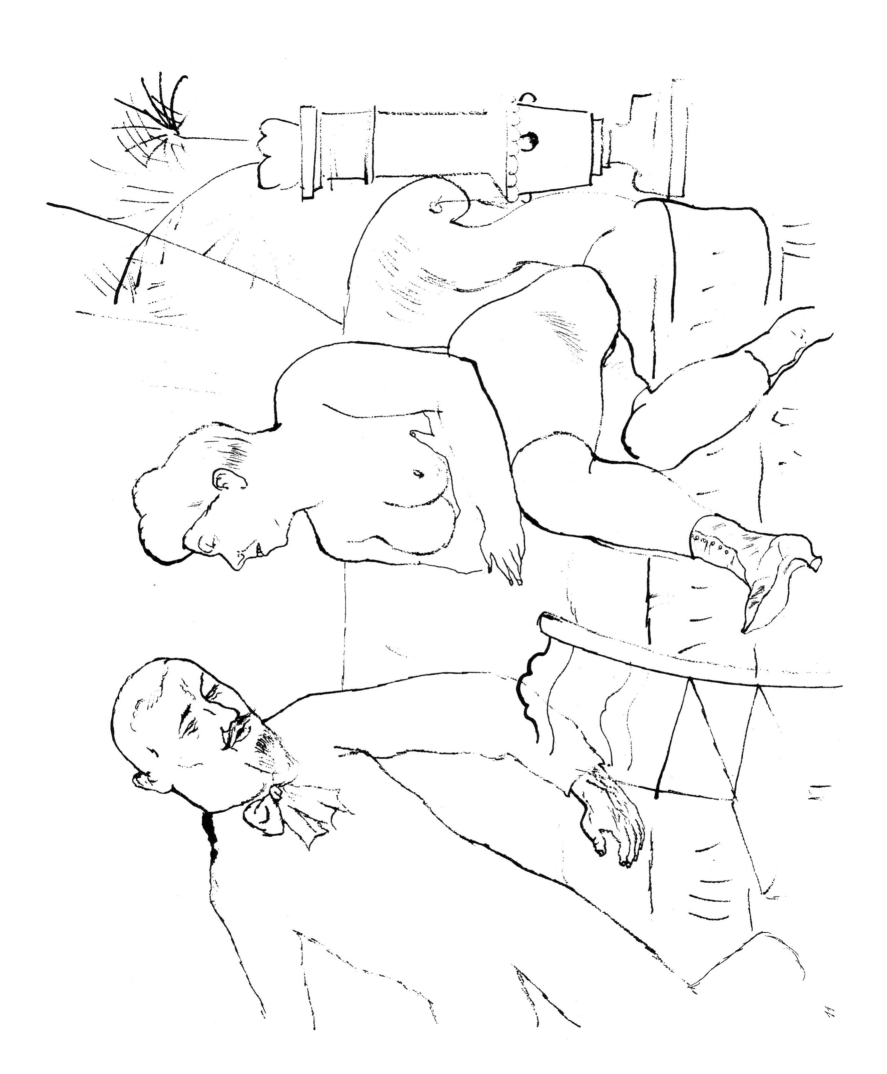

12

13

IV

16

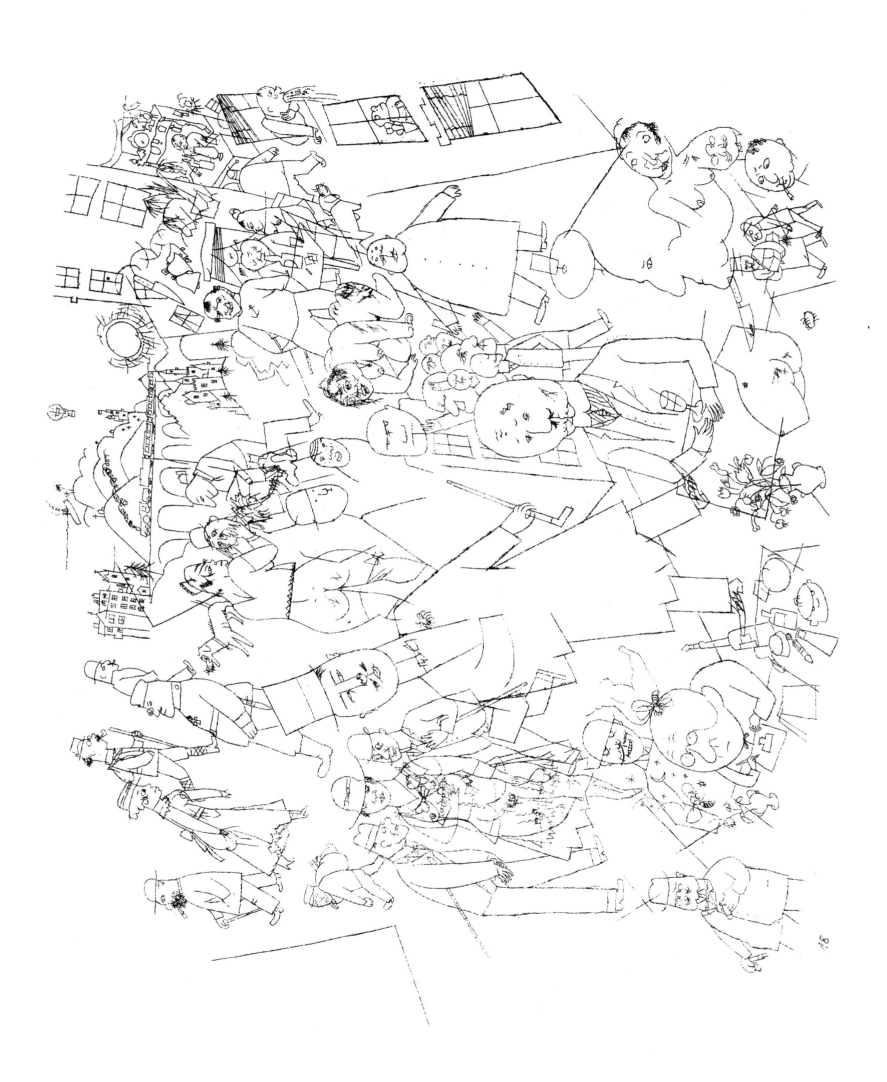

19

Frau Mertens John
Heartfield 1919

21

22

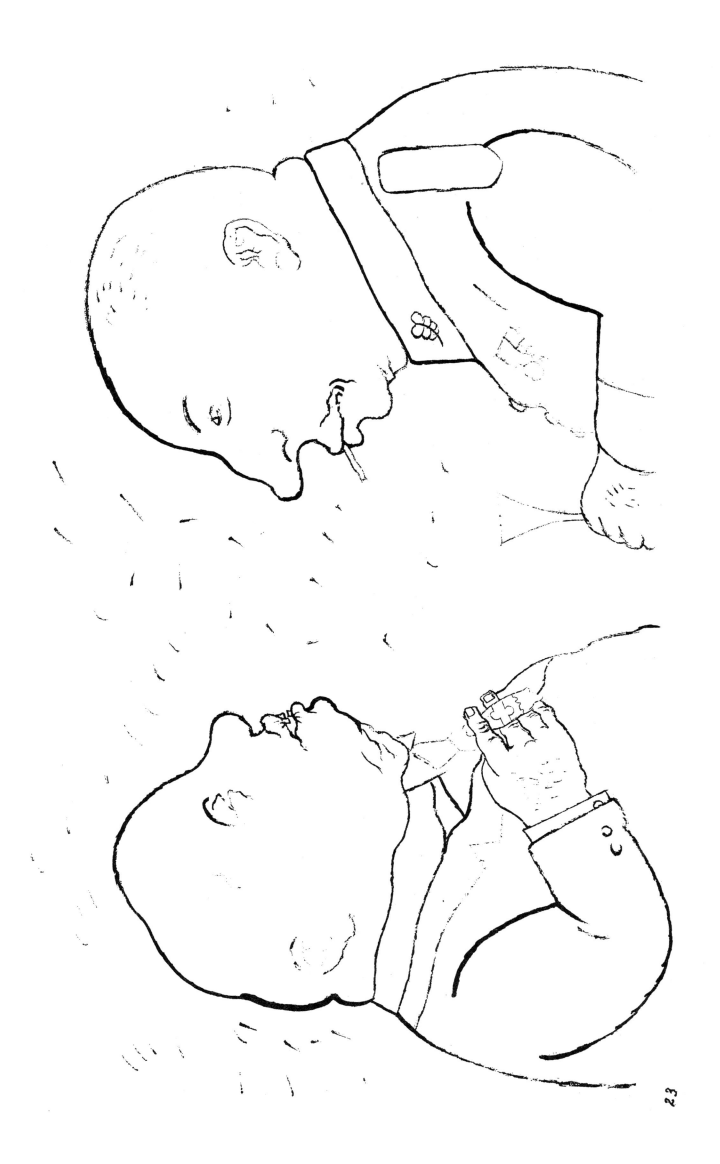

23

24

2,5

26

VI

27

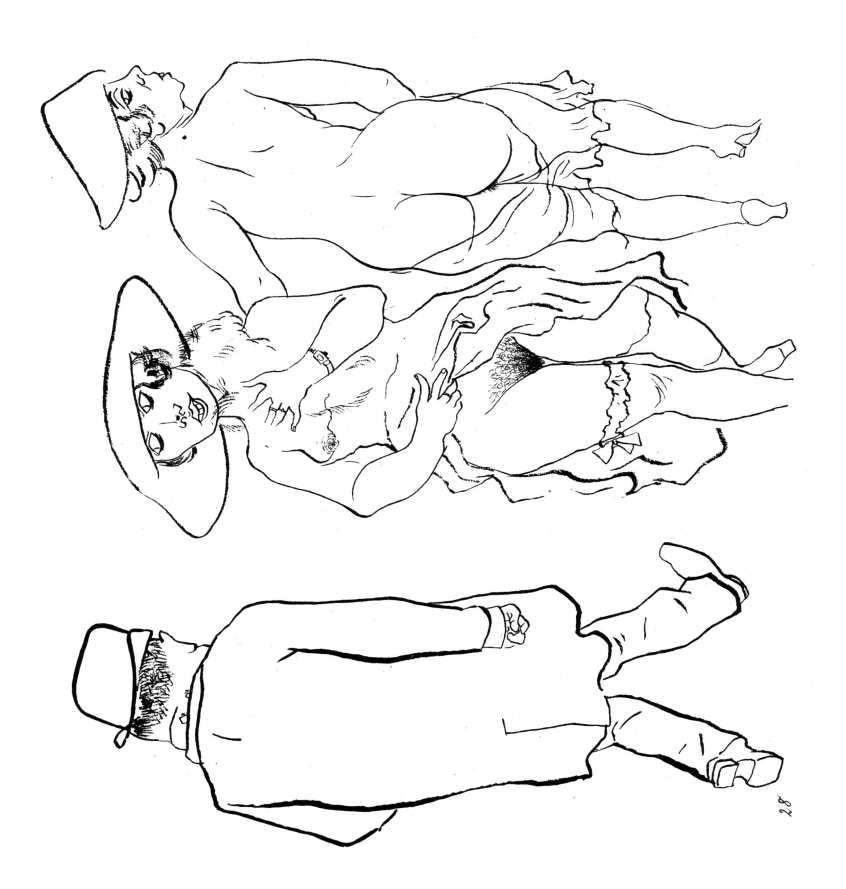

28

29

30

VII

31

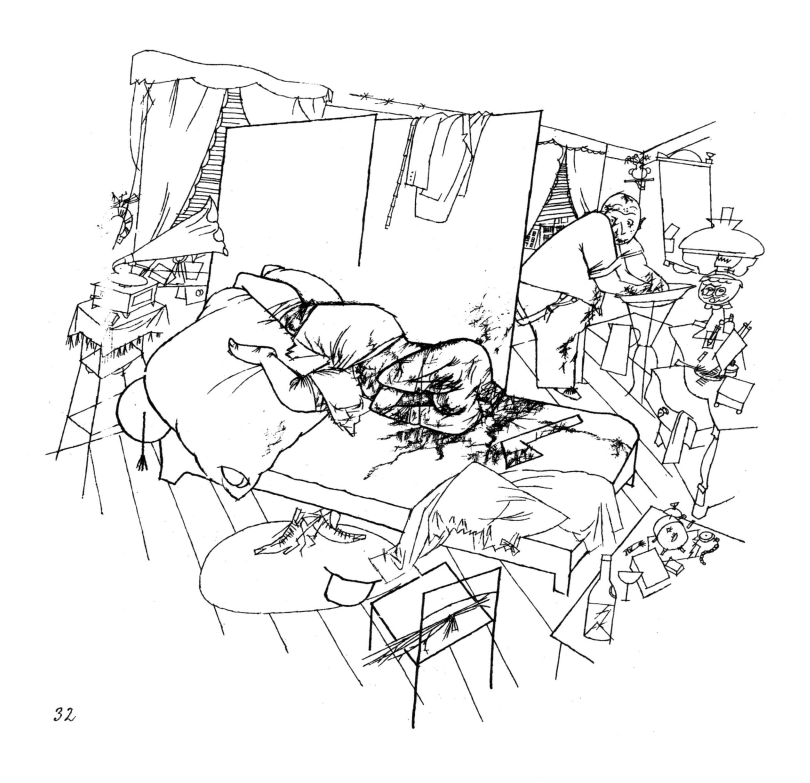

32

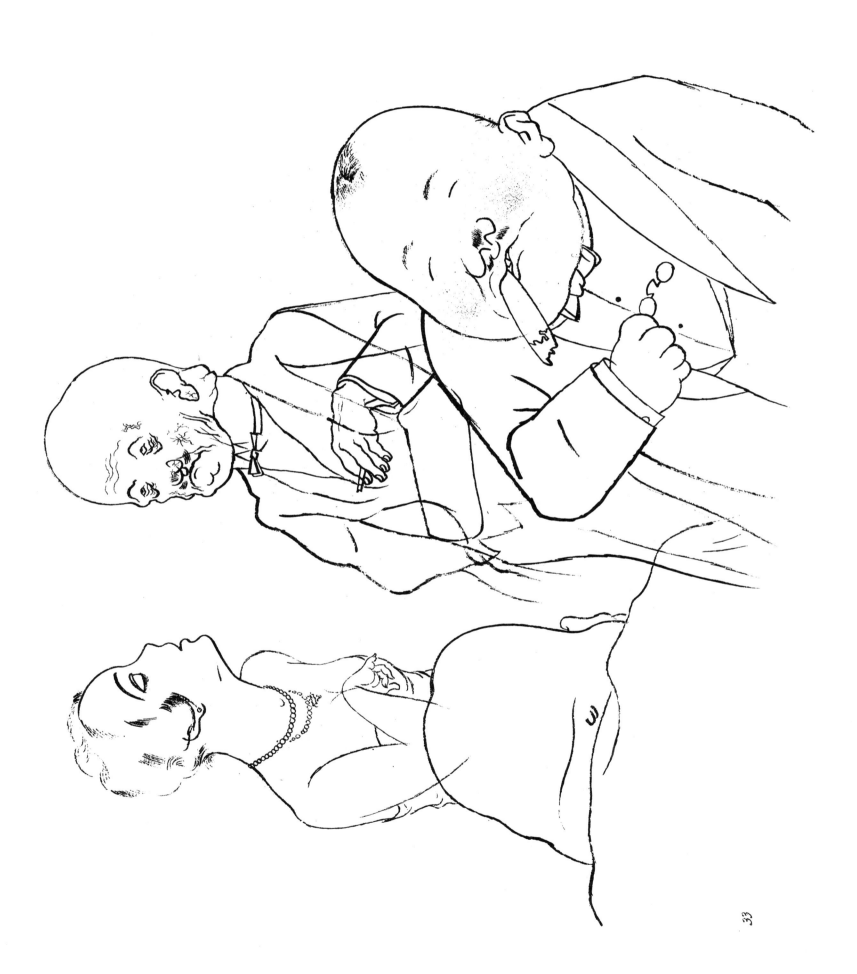

33

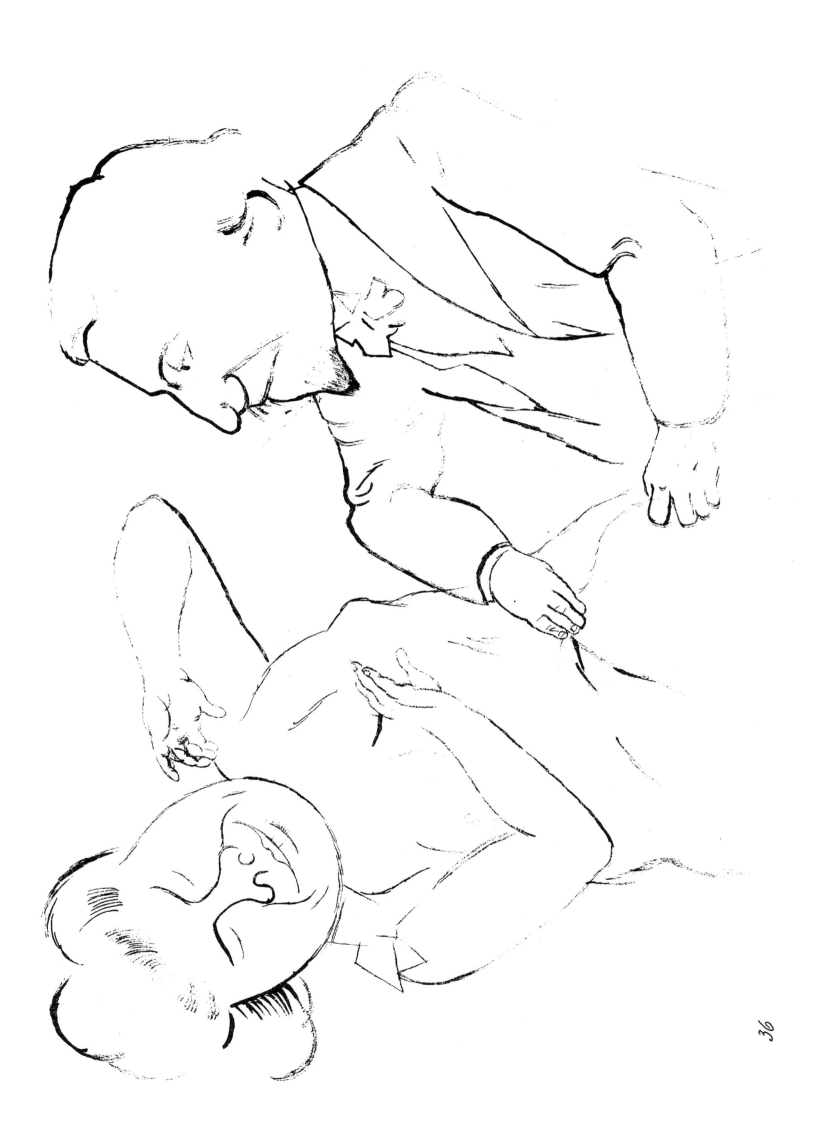

36

37

38

VIII

39

40

41

DR. DÜHREN
SADISMUS
und
MASOCHISMUS

42

IX

43

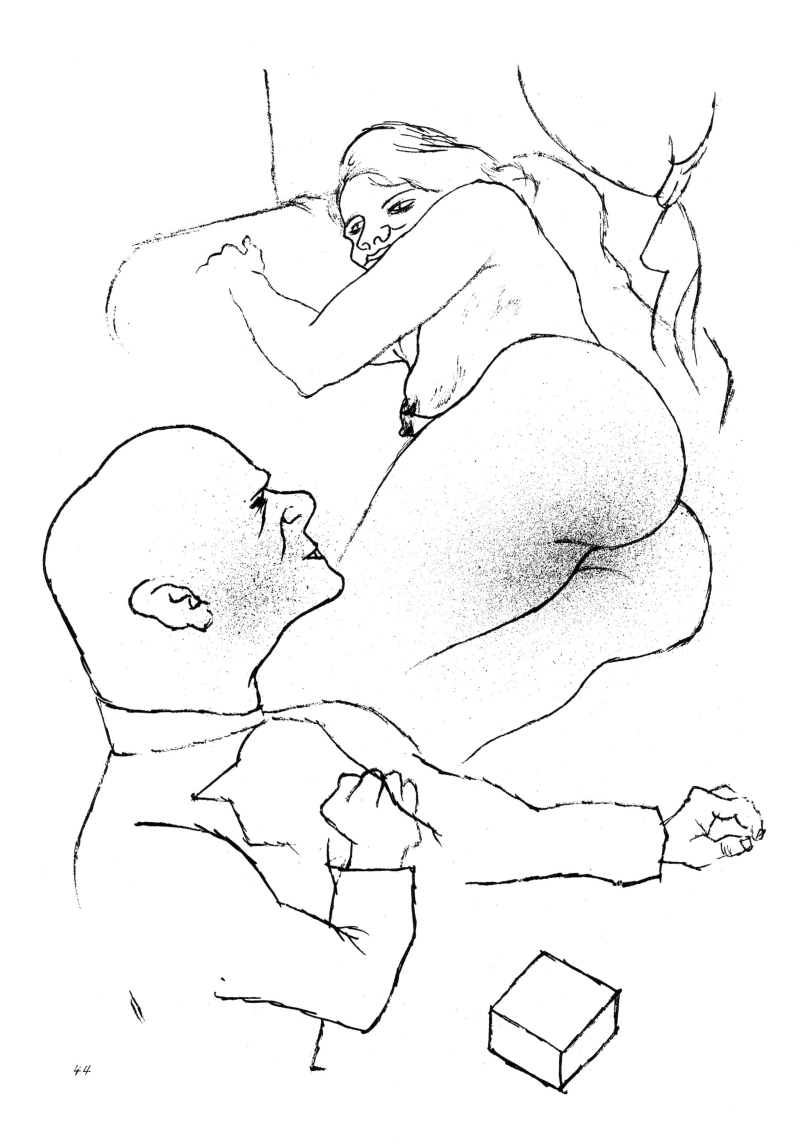

44

46

X

47

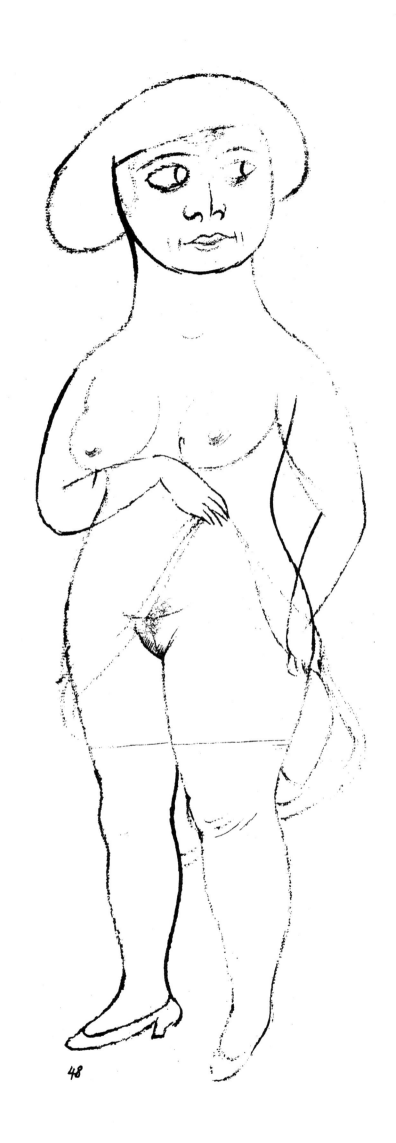

48

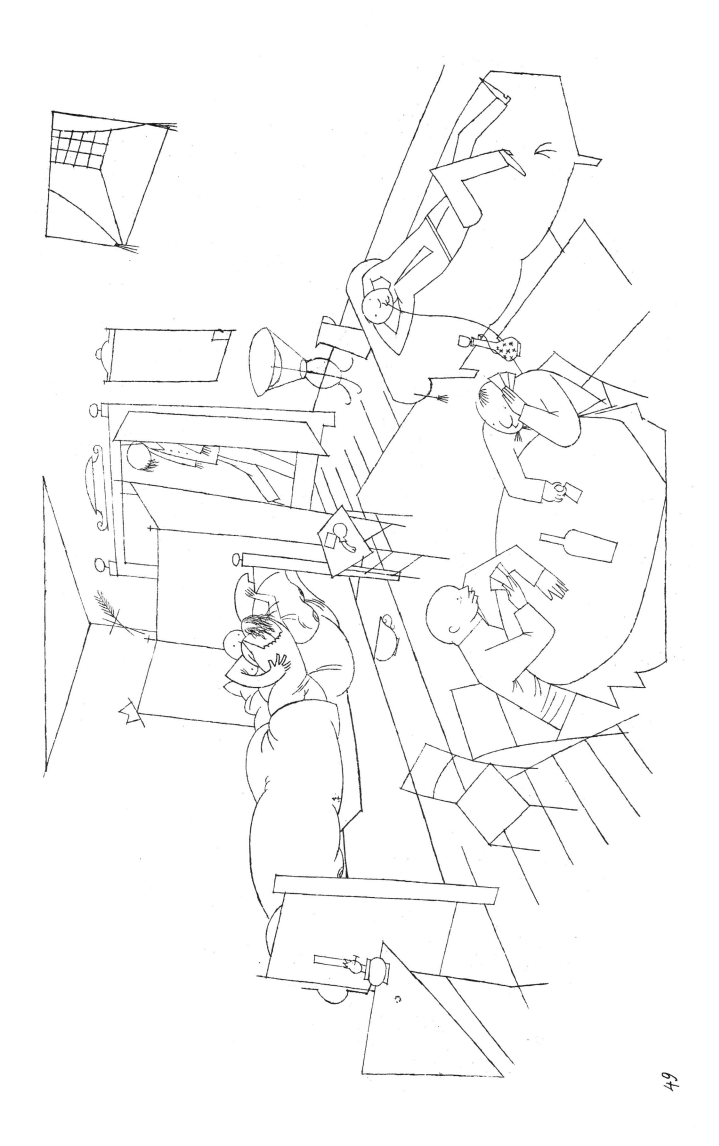

49

50

51

52

53

54

XI

55

56

58

XII

59

60

61

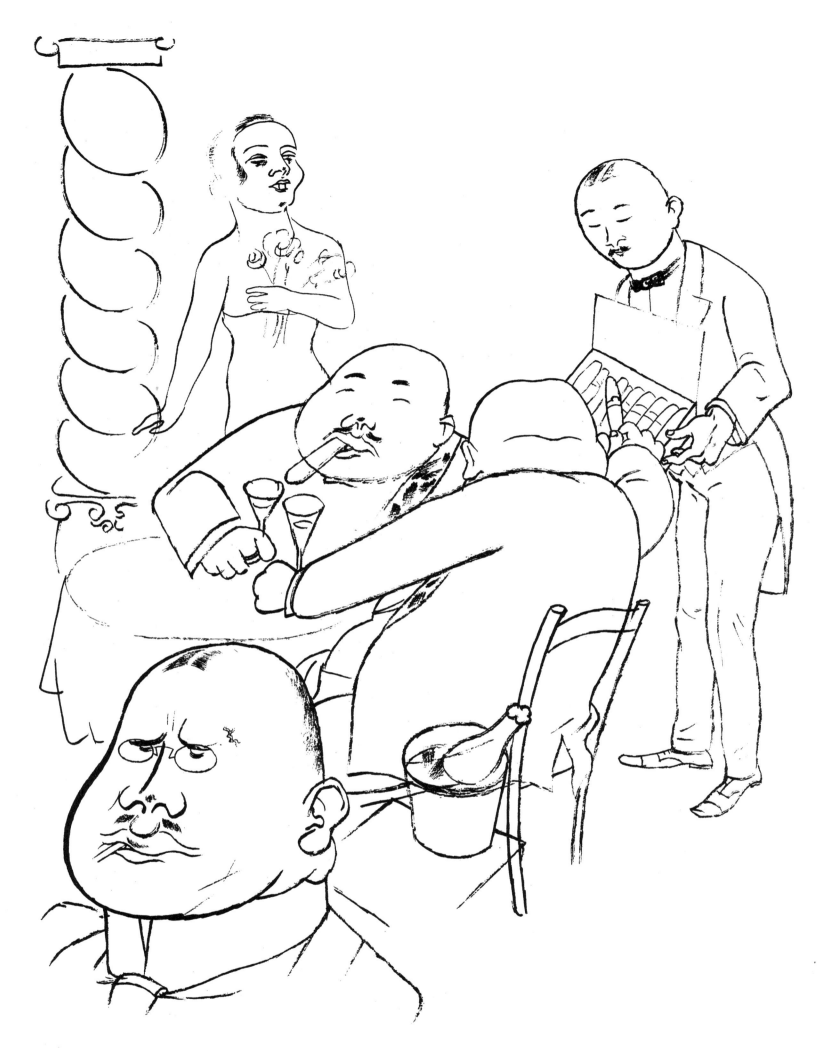

62

XIII

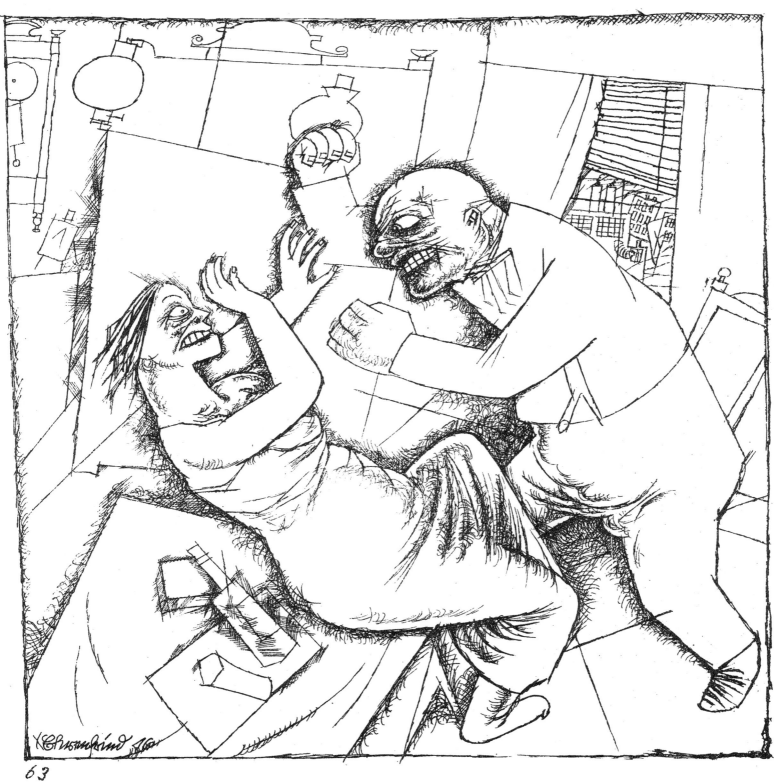

63

64

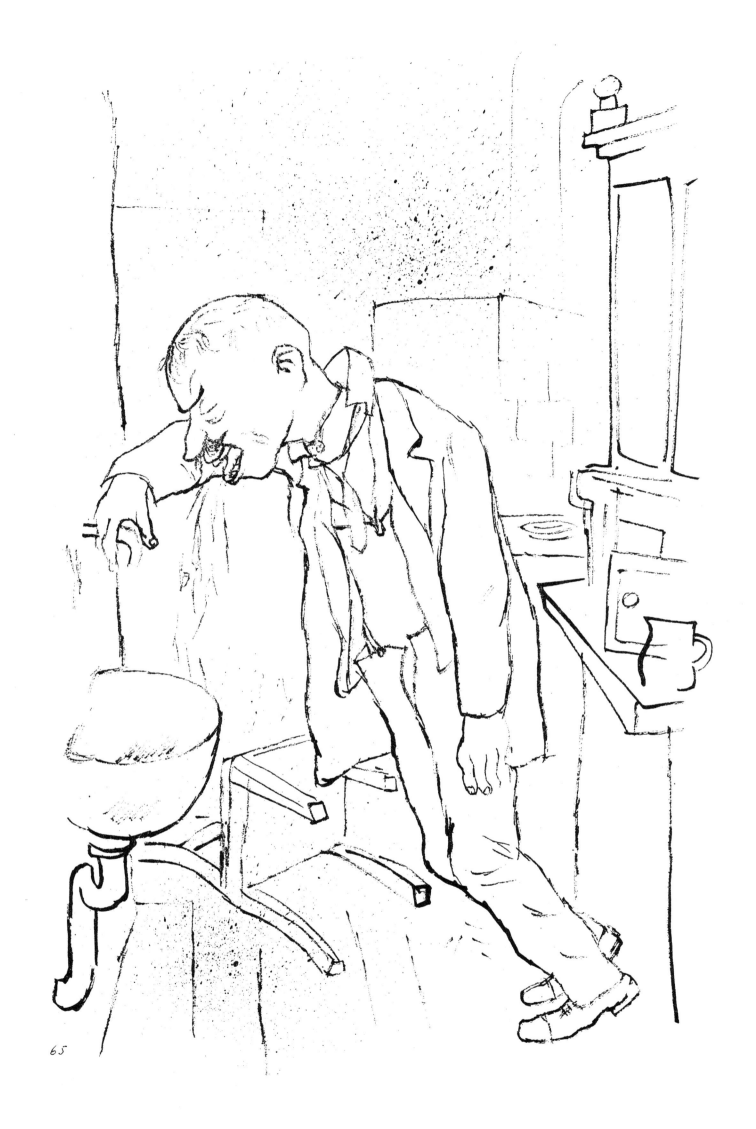

65

67

69

XIV

71

73

74

XV

75

77

78

XVI

79

80

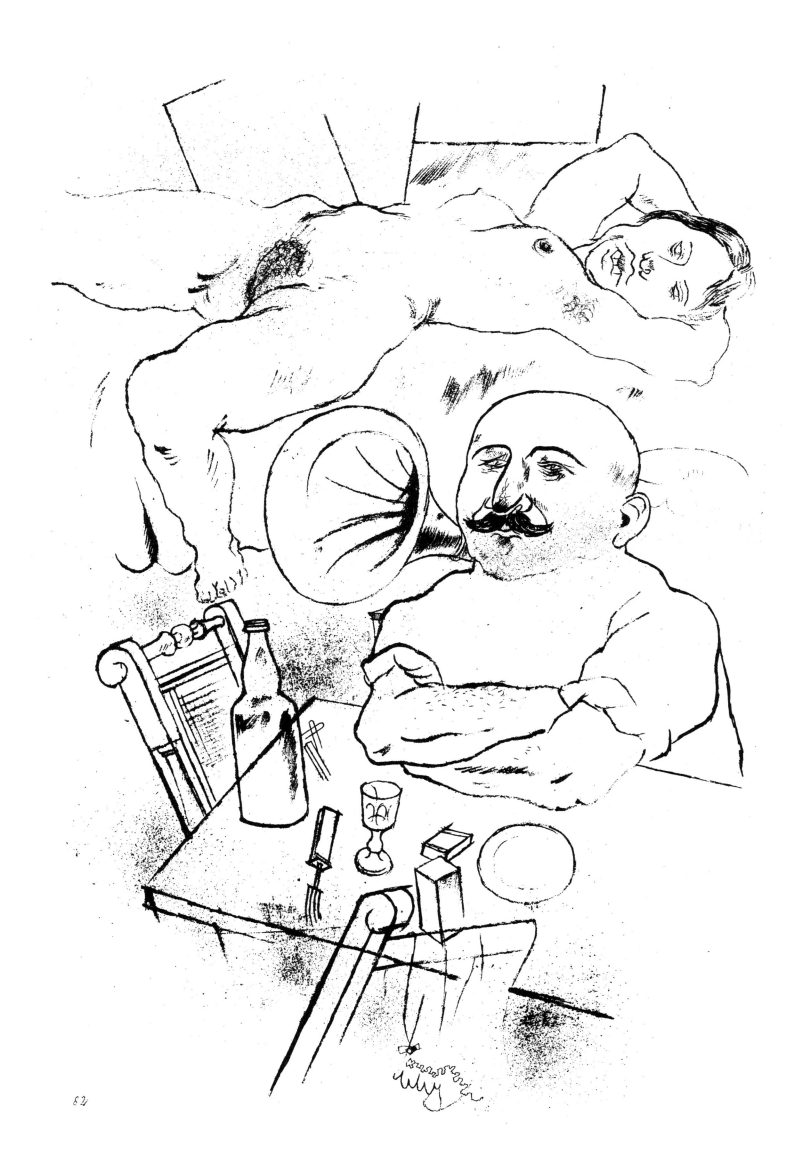

83

ECCE HOMO

Historical Note:

In 1923, legal action was brought against GEORGE GROSZ for issuing ECCO HOMO. This was based on a law that had not been evoked in centuries. The charge: defaming public morals, corrupting the inborn sense of shame and virtue innate in the German people. Grosz was found guilty, ordered to pay a fine of 6000 marks; and 24 of the plates were confiscated and banned from publication.

This edition faithfully follows the uncensored original issue, and contains all the illustrations of Grosz' masterwork.